RACEIN
AMERICA

RACE AND
ECONOMICS

BY M. M. EBOCH

CONTENT CONSULTANT
Tabitha Knight, PhD
Assistant Professor of Economics
Willamette University

ABDOPUBLISHING.COM

Published by Abdo Publishing, a division of ABDO, PO Box 398166, Minneapolis, Minnesota 55439. Copyright © 2018 by Abdo Consulting Group, Inc. International copyrights reserved in all countries. No part of this book may be reproduced in any form without written permission from the publisher. Essential Library™ is a trademark and logo of Abdo Publishing

Printed in the United States of America, North Mankato, Minnesota
052017
092017

Interior Photos: IP Galanternik D.U./iStockphoto, 4–5; Nam Y. Huh/ AP Images, 7; Aaron Huey/ National Geographic/Getty Images, 9; Jan Sucko/iStockphoto, 14–15; Shutterstock Images, 17; Ric Francis/ AP Images, 19; Hulton Archive/Getty Images, 23; Sam Myers/AP Images, 25; Atlanta Journal-Constitution/AP Images, 29; Bettmann/ Getty Images, 30; ullstein bild/Getty Images, 33; AP Images, 36; iStockphoto, 41, 52–53, 56, 61, 76–77, 82, 85, 88–89; Monkey Business Images/iStockphoto, 44, 46; M. Spencer Green/AP Images, 49; Nick Ut/AP Images, 58; Yuri Arcurs/iStockphoto, 64–65; Andrey Popov/ iStockphoto, 68; Carlos Osorio/AP Images, 72; Charles Bennett/AP Images, 75; Sergi Reboredo/VWPics/AP Images, 79; Seth Wenig/AP Images, 91; Andrew D. Brosig/The Daily Sentinel/AP Images, 92–93

Editor: Heidi Hogg
Series Designer: Maggie Villaume

PUBLISHER'S CATALOGING-IN-PUBLICATION DATA

Names: Eboch, M. M., author.
Title: Race and economics / by M. M. Eboch.
Description: Minneapolis, MN : Abdo Publishing, 2018. | Series: Race in America | Includes bibliographical references and index.
Identifiers: LCCN 2016962257 | ISBN 9781532110344 (lib. bdg.) | ISBN 9781680788198 (ebook)
Subjects: LCSH: Race--Juvenile literature. | Economic conditions--Juvenile literature.
Classification: DDC 305.8--dc23
LC record available at http://lccn.loc.gov/2016962257

CONTENTS

CHAPTER ONE
STARTING POINTS
4

CHAPTER TWO
ECONOMICS AND HISTORY
14

CHAPTER THREE
RACISM IN AMERICAN SOCIETY
30

CHAPTER FOUR
GETTING A HEALTHY START
40

CHAPTER FIVE
EDUCATION AND CAREER OPPORTUNITIES
52

CHAPTER SIX
NETWORKING FOR WORK
64

CHAPTER SEVEN
DIVERSITY CHALLENGES
76

CHAPTER EIGHT
THE FUTURE
88

ESSENTIAL FACTS   100   SOURCE NOTES   106

GLOSSARY   102   INDEX   110

ADDITIONAL RESOURCES   104   ABOUT THE AUTHOR   112

CHAPTER ONE

STARTING POINTS

The United States is often thought of as a land of opportunity, where anyone who works hard enough can achieve success. This success is typically defined in economic terms: the ability to get a good job at a good income, or to start a business that makes a profit. Hard work certainly increases an individual's chance of economic success. Yet success is far easier for some individuals and groups than for others, as the following fictional case studies demonstrate.

Emma lives in a middle-income suburb. Even before she was born, her parents worked to give her the best possible life. Her mother took vitamins while pregnant to keep her growing baby healthy. Emma sees a doctor often and gets all the recommended vaccines and tests. Her house is full of books, and her parents have been reading to her since she was born.

Emma's school is ranked as one of the best in the state. She has attentive teachers, classrooms well stocked with supplies, and choices of after-school activities. Emma has a slight learning disability, which might have caused her to struggle in school. However, it was diagnosed early, and she received extensive tutoring. Now she is on track to graduate at the top of her class. She will probably receive a scholarship to college, but if not, her parents can afford

Schools in middle- and upper-income neighborhoods often have amenities such as modern cafeterias and large swimming pools.

to pay for her to attend. After she finishes college, she will be able to draw on her parents' extensive network of colleagues to help in her job search. Maybe she will become a businesswoman, a doctor, a scientist, or an artist — her choices seem endless.

Shawn lives in poverty. He grew up in an old apartment building that has not been remodeled since the 1970s. The walls are covered in flaking, lead-based paint. The pipes that carry his drinking water are also made of lead. When he breathes, eats, or drinks particles of this lead, they affect his health. Lead can lower one's IQ and cause behavior and learning problems, hyperactivity, and hearing damage.

Shawn's teacher is overwhelmed by dozens of kids in an overcrowded classroom, so she has no time to give Shawn individual attention. In a high-crime community, the first priority of teachers and administrators at school is keeping order. Providing a good education falls second to maintaining discipline. Shawn's mother works two jobs, so she does not have time to help him with his homework. In any case, she dropped out of high school and can barely read because her own learning disability was never diagnosed. They have no books in their home. Few of their friends or neighbors went to college or have professional jobs. Shawn doesn't know if he will be able to graduate from high school. He has no dreams of college, because he has few examples of people furthering their education.

Raquel lives in a two-room house with her grandparents, mother, two siblings, and a cousin. The home is too hot in the summer and too cold in the winter. Family members have to get water from a pump at a nearby well. They use gas lamps because they have no electricity. They do not

CHILDREN AND POVERTY

In 2013, there were 14.7 million children living in poverty in the United States—20 percent of all US children. While the overall poverty rate for children has been declining since 2010, the rate for black children has remained largely unchanged. Furthermore, black children are much more likely to live in poverty than their nonblack peers. In 2013, 38 percent of black children lived in poverty. This is nearly three times the rate for white children. Hispanic children were also much more likely to live in poverty, with a rate of 30 percent.[1]

have telephones either. Raquel's family lives miles from any doctors. A local oil company uses a legal loophole and dumps wastewater near the river, which is causing health problems in the people who live nearby. Raquel rarely sees her father, who had to move to a larger city to find work. He sends money home, but it is hardly enough to support the extended family.

Many adults and children in the community are alcoholics or drug users. Crime is high, with little law enforcement to combat it. Raquel does not know anyone who has gone to college. Only half of her classmates will graduate from high school. She can hardly imagine a future other than what she already knows.

THE FACTOR OF RACE

Many people think of race as skin color, but the term can also include other factors such as religion and place of

American Indian children live in poverty on a reservation in South Dakota.

WHAT IS POVERTY?

In 2016, the poverty threshold for a family of two adults and two children was $24,339.[3] This figure is determined by the US Census Bureau. The organization arrives at that number by calculating how much it should cost to feed a family of four and then multiplies that number by three; that is, two-thirds of a family's income should go to expenses other than food. However, as many economists have pointed out, this does not accurately reflect spending in today's society and fails to incorporate the rising costs of other basic needs, such as housing, clothing, transportation, child care, and medical care. The process does not take into account regional differences either.

origin. Racism is the belief that some races are better or worse than others. In theory, each of the young people in the fictional case studies could be of any race. But in practice, Emma is most likely to be white, and Shawn is more likely African American. Meanwhile, Raquel may be an American Indian living on a reservation. In 2015, 9.1 percent of non-Hispanic white Americans lived in poverty, along with 11.4 percent of Asian Americans. In contrast, 24.1 percent of African Americans and 21.4 percent of Hispanics lived in poverty.[2]

The percentage of African Americans and Hispanics living in poverty decreased in 2015 compared to 2014. Still, ten million African Americans and more than 12 million Hispanics lived in poverty. The number of non-Hispanic whites living in poverty was 17.8 million. While this number is higher overall, it is a smaller percentage because non-Hispanic whites make up more than 60 percent of the total US population.[4]

As of 2008, 28.2 percent of American Indians lived below the federal poverty line.[5] The percentage was even higher for those living on reservations. Houses on reservations are often overcrowded, and approximately one in ten lacks access to safe drinking water. Fewer than 10 percent of homes have Internet access. American Indians have the lowest employment rate of any US racial or ethnic group. In some American Indian communities, unemployment is as high as 85 percent. High school graduation rates are among the lowest as well, often dipping below 50 percent.[6]

AMERICAN INDIAN LEGACY

In 2013, President Barack Obama noted, "The painful legacy of discrimination means that . . . Native Americans are far more likely to suffer from a lack of opportunity—higher unemployment, (and) higher poverty rates."[7] Similar to African Americans, American Indians are still suffering from an early history of subjugation. Their land was taken by European immigrants, usually through violence, theft, or broken treaties. American Indian nations were often forced to move to less-desirable locations. They suffered forced assimilation, with children sent to schools where they were not allowed to speak their language or practice their culture. These circumstances affected their current economic opportunities.

Centuries of racism have contributed to this situation. Technically, laws prohibit discrimination based on race, color, national origin, religion, and sex. These laws cover employment in the state and federal governments, private businesses with at least 15 employees, and some other organizations. Meanwhile, schools that receive federal financial assistance may not discriminate based on race, color, or national origin. This covers the vast majority of public school districts and public colleges and universities, as well as many private colleges and universities.

Under the law, everyone should be treated equally and have an equal chance to get a good education, find a good job, and be paid well. However, in reality, laws alone have not been

THE TRUTH ABOUT UNEMPLOYMENT

The unemployment rate is usually defined as the percentage of the total labor force that is actively seeking employment and is willing to work but not employed. The real unemployment rate is likely even higher. People are considered unemployed only if they are actively looking for work. Someone who cannot find work may eventually stop looking, at which point he or she is no longer counted in the unemployment statistics.

Unemployment statistics vary among different racial groups. Unemployment rates tend to go down as a person completes more education. But for every level of educational attainment, such as high school graduation, an associate's degree, or a bachelor's degree, the unemployment rate for African Americans consistently remains close to twice that of their white counterparts.

enough to erase centuries of racist policies. Educational funding tends to keep richer communities successful and prevent students in poor communities from getting out of poverty. In addition, children in poverty are more likely to have undiagnosed health problems and learning disabilities. They receive less help with homework, and they see fewer examples of educational advancement and financial success. Race also affects income, housing, medical care, and even life expectancy. Minorities of all ages have more difficulty accessing health care and receiving quality care. Childhood health affects success in school, and poor health in adults can interfere with people's ability to work. Unequal access to health care therefore helps to keep poor families in poverty. And because poverty is tied to race, race is still a factor in economic success in America.

| DISCUSSION STARTERS |

- How do racist policies of centuries past affect people today?

- Do you believe race and poverty are related? Why or why not?

- What is unequal access, and how might it contribute to keeping some people in poverty?

CHAPTER TWO

ECONOMICS
AND HISTORY

The field of economics is concerned with the production, use, and transfer of wealth. This includes the production, buying, selling, and other transfer of merchandise and services, as well as their consumption or use. Economists study the world around them. They ask questions about what they observe. Economists then collect and study data, developing economic theories to try to answer their questions. The information economists study may involve home prices, consumer spending, or unemployment rates. They use the collected information to make and test predictions about how people and financial markets will behave. Studying how economics and racism interact provides insight into both racial and financial issues.

Economics can help explain why some people or groups grow richer while others grow poorer. It can explore why wealth has become more unequally distributed in the United States. It can make predictions about what jobs may be available in the future, whether the educational system is preparing people properly, and who is most likely to succeed in those jobs.

Few economic studies include race as a factor. However, considering race can help economists understand how much race and racism affect people's finances and opportunities. In addition, understanding how race plays a factor in economics could help those who are privileged recognize the advantages they have been given.

Economists study issues both small and large, from the choices of individuals to those of businesses, banks, and governments. Some studies explore how and why people decide to spend or save their money. Others look at when and how the world economy improves or falters. Studies might look at how trends such as increased immigration affect the economy. Economists may predict how government programs, such as health insurance subsidies or changes in tax law, will affect people.

Economists use data to study trends and make predictions about the future.

MULTIPLE MARKETS

A market is any place where two or more people exchange goods and services. This includes local stores that sell goods to customers, such as supermarkets. An exchange of services could be the job agreement between an employee and an employer. Contracts between individuals such as a homeowner and a plumber or a car owner and a mechanic are other examples. Markets also include large businesses that sell to other businesses.

The market system, also referred to simply as the market, includes all these markets and others. The market system is the overall framework within which people make economic choices. No one created or controls this market system. However, the government plays a role in maintaining it. For example, the government can pass laws to ensure that people can legally own and exchange property. Laws can enforce contracts and make it illegal to use threats or violence to force someone to buy or sell goods and services. However, these laws are effective only if they are enforced.

SUPPLY AND DEMAND

While economics may seem to revolve around money, the subject is broader than that. Up until a few hundred years ago, many people believed the value of an item depended solely on the cost it took to produce it. They believed an item's value was fixed. For example, the value of a shirt should be based on the cost of making it. However, most economists no longer hold this belief. Modern economists point out that people are sometimes willing to pay much more for an item than it should be worth. That's because the value of an object is influenced by supply and demand. Demand is based on what consumers want and need, as well as their ability to pay for an object. If demand for an item or service increases, its price will go up. This encourages more businesses to start producing that item or offering that service. If demand decreases, prices go down and fewer businesses offer that item or service. Over time, supply should rise or decrease to meet the population's demand.

The value of an item is also affected by scarcity. When an item is scarce, there is a limited supply of it. Economists study how scarce items are distributed across members of a population. They also study how people's behavior changes when they have too little of something.

Gasoline prices tend to increase in the summer months when more people drive.

SCHOOLS OF THOUGHT

Economists are individuals whose experiences and perceptions vary. This leads different economists to ask different questions about the world and use different theories to try to predict what will happen. For example, neoclassical economists assert that people are inherently selfish. They will make economic decisions to maximize their individual well-being. This theory also states that people will behave rationally to get what they want. For example, think of a manager hiring a new employee. According to neoclassical economists, the manager will always hire the most qualified individual, because doing so will likely increase the manager's wealth.

WHAT IS WEALTH?

Wealth is not the same thing as income. Annual income is the amount of money a person earns in one year. Wealth is the sum of a person's assets with debt subtracted. For example, think of a bathtub. The water coming out of the faucet is income. Any water going down the drain is debt. The water that remains in the tub is wealth.

Wealth is important because it allows a person to set aside income to pay for future expenses. Wealth also protects a person during times of economic insecurity, such as unemployment. African Americans have not had the same opportunities to build wealth as white people have, and the current disparity of wealth between racial groups is stark. According to the Economic Policy Institute, the average wealth for white families was seven times higher than the average wealth for black families in 2013.[1]

Political economic theory offers many alternatives to neoclassical theory. While there are differences among the various theories, political economists study how politics, sociology, and culture are linked to economics. Political economists also assume there are more factors at play than a person's selfish economic interests. For example, political economists believe managers consider factors such as race and gender when making hiring decisions. Neoclassical economists would classify such behavior as irrational, but political economists argue it may be in a manager's best interests to ensure his or her hiring practices reflect the current social environment, even at the risk of economic hardship.

Most people want money, but they may want other things even more. For example, some parents may take jobs that pay less but allow their families to live in good school districts, thus allowing their children to receive a good education. Someone else might take a job that pays less but offers more flexibility, enabling the person to care for an ill family member or young children. Other people prioritize factors such as the size of the city or town, the activities available, or even the climate. People are complex, especially when they interact with other people or systems. Economics is constantly evolving as economists learn more and develop new theories.

STUDYING HISTORY

History provides real-world case studies to show whether human behavior matches what economists predict. Studying the past in economic terms can help people understand the history of racism. In fact, studying discrimination and economics has revealed some surprises. People have not always behaved in the way most economists thought they would.

Before the American Civil War (1861–1865), race clearly affected people's economic potential. An enslaved person had fewer opportunities than a free person. But when enslaved people were freed, classic economic theory predicted market forces would eliminate most racist behavior. In a free market, prices and wages are determined by competition. Buyers and sellers can make any arrangements they wish. The forces of supply and demand determine how much people are willing to pay for goods or services.

By this theory, people who behave in racist ways should suffer financially. For example, employers who refuse to hire African Americans have a smaller labor pool. Therefore, they might have to pay more to get good employees. Likewise, labor unions, which depend on workers banding together to make demands on employers, will have fewer members if they admit only people of a

Prior to the 1960s, some stores were openly racist with regard to the customers they served.

certain race. For instance, a whites-only union cannot control the workers outside the union. Those nonwhite workers might fill jobs when the union goes on strike, giving the union less leverage.

Racist small businesses and individuals ought to suffer as well, according to neoclassical theory. If a store refuses to sell to people of a certain race, it could lose business. A restaurant that serves only white people will lose many potential customers. People with houses on the market who refuse to sell to African American families might lose buyers willing to pay the highest price. Because of these factors, racism should have been a financial disadvantage.

CONTROLLING FREEDOM

The free market turned out to be less free than predicted. In an ideal free market, the government does not take part in controlling prices or wages. However, when one segment of the population has power, those people may pass laws to their own benefit.

In the South after the Civil War, white plantation owners quickly worked to reassert their power. They passed a series of laws that applied only to African Americans. These became known as Jim Crow laws. When these laws were in effect, African Americans were allowed to work only in certain jobs. This kept black and white workers from competing against one another. These laws enforced segregation in other ways, too. Black and white people were not allowed to share public facilities. They had separate schools, libraries, hospitals, hotels, restaurants, bathrooms, and drinking fountains. By 1910, all Southern states had laws that kept African Americans (and many poor whites) from voting. Several cities had laws that restricted where African Americans could live. These laws lasted until the civil rights movement of the 1960s.

In the North, many neighborhoods and schools remained segregated for decades. As black people moved into northern cities, white people moved to the suburbs.

Some new communities, such as Levittown, New York, sold homes only to white people. Many Northern shopkeepers displayed "whites only" signs. Businesses openly practiced discrimination, hiring white people exclusively. Northern federal courts typically denied

Neighbors protested when a black family moved to Levittown in 1957.

CHINESE IMMIGRANTS

Racist policies and prejudice affected immigrants as well as American-born people of color. Chinese people began arriving in California in large numbers in the 1850s. They faced social prejudice and legal restrictions when looking for work. In 1865, the Central Pacific Railroad needed more workers. When it could not find enough white men to do the grueling labor, the company reluctantly hired some Chinese workers. The Chinese employees did so well that the railroad started advertising in China to attract more workers. By 1868, the railroad had more than 12,000 Chinese workers, which was at least 80 percent of its workforce.[2] The other workers, mostly Irish men, often resented the competition from the Chinese, even though the Irish workers received more money for less-dangerous jobs.

The Chinese railroad workers faced many hardships and dangers, and more than 1,000 died in accidents and avalanches.[3] Despite their contribution to the country's infrastructure, discrimination against the Chinese in the United States continued for generations.

any legal challenges to these practices.

Racism was strongest where ethnic groups competed most closely. After the Civil War, many freed black people moved north and began to compete against white people for jobs. This competition increased negative feelings. Competition arose between different white ethnic groups as well. For example, white people born in the United States with English ancestry were often prejudiced against more recent immigrants of the mid-1800s, particularly the Irish. The recent immigrants could often find employment only by taking low-paying jobs. But newly freed African Americans were also competing for these jobs. Whenever one group felt financially threatened by another group, prejudice and racist behavior increased. For instance, in New York City after the Civil War, many Irish people worked in factories or domestic service, which were among the few jobs open to them. To protect their jobs, they blocked attempts by African Americans and Chinese immigrants to gain employment. History shows that rather than promoting free-market equality, the abolishment of slavery did little to end racism.

| DISCUSSION STARTERS |

- How and why does the study of economics go beyond money?

- How do you think a free-market economy can work toward eliminating racism? Why do you think this has not been achieved in practice?

- Why do you think people created racist laws and policies that kept others from having an equal opportunity for economic success?

VOTER
SUPPRESSION|

Legally, African American men received the right to vote on February 3, 1870, according to the Fifteenth Amendment to the US Constitution. However, in practice, few African Americans in southern states were allowed to vote before 1965. Southern states passed laws that specifically targeted African Americans. Some laws said only people who could read were allowed to vote. Before the Civil War, it was illegal for enslaved black people to learn to read or write. Many freedmen were illiterate, but so were many poor white people. White officials sometimes allowed illiterate white people to vote but denied that right to black people who could read.

Other laws required people to own property in order to vote. Because a disproportionate number of landowners were white, this law was discriminatory against black people. In addition, white officials sometimes purged voting rolls, removing the names of registered voters, particularly African Americans. People might arrive at the polls to discover they were no longer registered to vote. African Americans who tried to vote were sometimes threatened with violence, fired from their jobs, or kicked off of their farms. Some had their homes burned down or their families hurt. Some were even killed for trying to vote.

Changes in the 1960s, including the Voting Rights Act passed by Congress in 1965, made many of these practices illegal. However, some laws still make it difficult for minorities to vote. Certain states require government-issued identification. Getting these IDs may require time and money, and may in some cases involve travel to distant offices. This is more difficult for poor people, the homeless, and those who do not own cars or find it hard to travel, such as the elderly.

The PRESENCE OF SEGREGATION IS THE ABSENCE OF DEMOCRACY JIM CROW MUST GO!

A protester speaks out about Jim Crow laws in 1961.

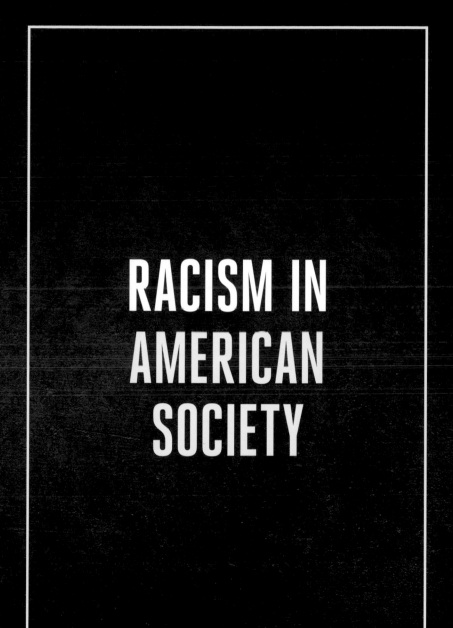

CHAPTER THREE

RACISM IN AMERICAN SOCIETY

World War I (1914–1918) changed the labor market in the United States. With many young men away fighting, businesses had fewer choices of workers. Some companies could no longer afford to hire only white employees; there simply weren't enough white men available. African American workers took some traditionally white positions. White women took some traditionally black positions. Many African Americans migrated north to take advantage of job opportunities in manufacturing. During World War I, the black population increased greatly in many northern cities.

When soldiers returned from the war, some companies went back to their previous practices, but others did not. Soldiers returned to an uncertain job market, with more people competing for jobs. White men, facing new job competition, turned to group racism. They formed cartels to protect their jobs and income. A cartel is a group that bands together for mutual benefit. Typically, the term is used for a group of businesses that agree not to compete with one another. The members of the cartel decide to charge the same prices. They may also limit competition by controlling the supply of a product to be sold.

White workers began behaving as cartels. When people work together as a group, they can limit competition from those outside the group. This is known as job competition effects. White unions would not admit nonwhites. Since some jobs were available only to union members, this kept those jobs off-limits to people of other races. Union jobs tended to pay higher wages, benefiting white families. Excluding minorities meant white men had a better chance of securing well-paid jobs.

Businesses benefited from racist policies as well. When workers competed with one another for jobs, they were not able to band together. For example, minorities struggled to have the same opportunities as white men. Because these groups were pitted against one another, they did not work together to increase wages for everyone.

During World War I, many factories had no choice but to hire nonwhite workers.

CHALLENGING CARTELS

By agreeing not to compete with other members, cartels create high prices for consumers. Consequently, cartels do not have an incentive to develop new or better products, as there is little competition. Starting in 1890, the US government began passing laws to eliminate cartels or monopolies. These laws were designed to encourage competition among businesses, which is generally good for consumers. In the United States, the European Union, and some other areas, cartels are now illegal. Punishments can include fines and even prison sentences. However, governments struggle to detect and stop cartels because a cartel typically makes agreements secretly.

The effects of this struggle meant businesses were then able to keep labor costs low.

RULE BY INTIMIDATION

Social threats help cartel groups enforce their demands. In cities such as Chicago, Illinois, homeowners' associations attempted to keep neighborhoods segregated by race prior to the Civil Rights Act of 1964. Association members sometimes harassed and threatened both buyers and sellers. White sellers were threatened if they tried to sell to a black family in a predominantly white neighborhood. They also faced social shame and economic boycotts.

One Chicago community used the local newspaper to publish the name, new address, and job of any white person who sold to a black buyer. The homeowners' association might refuse to do business with or socialize with that person. If an African American family did buy a house, the homeowners' association used threats and violence to make them leave. Tactics included burning crosses on lawns, firing guns at the houses, breaking in to ransack homes, and threatening murder.

Community laws and regulations often encouraged these practices. This is how the poverty cycle is perpetuated. For example, in some cities, real estate boards and banks refused loans to African Americans. These practices might hurt an

CROSS BURNING

Today, burning crosses are associated with racist violence—specifically the Ku Klux Klan (KKK), a white supremacist organization. However, the practice dates back to medieval Europe, when Scottish clans set fire to crosses on hillsides. They used the bright flames to rally troops to battle or show defiance toward rivals.

The Ku Klux Klan, founded in 1866, did not initially use burning crosses. The practice is described in a 1905 novel, *The Clansman*, which supports racial segregation. Author Thomas Dixon was trying to give the KKK legitimacy by connecting it to Scottish clan traditions. The book was made into a movie, *The Birth of a Nation*, ten years later. Klansmen began using burning crosses to intimidate minorities and anyone else who challenged their ideals.

Even in recent decades, people have used cross burning to intimidate minorities. By some estimates, 30 to 50 cross burnings happen every year in the United States.[1]

individual home seller, who had a more limited choice of buyers. However, the white community benefited as a whole. Since many white people wanted to live in exclusively white neighborhoods, house prices stayed higher. Because white people typically had the best jobs, white neighborhoods tended to be wealthier. Wealthy neighborhoods had better public facilities, such as schools and sanitation systems. This kept the next generation of white children healthier and better educated.

Members of the Ku Klux Klan, dressed in white robes, burn a cross at a rally.

Middle-income black families, in contrast, were discouraged from living in communities with white neighbors in the same income bracket. Instead, many lived alongside low-income black families. Their children, although coming from middle-income parents, went to schools with fewer resources than their white peers. Limited access to quality education then limited the job opportunities available to them.

DISCRIMINATION AND ECONOMICS

In 1955, economist Gary Becker wrote about discrimination. According to Becker, the free-market economy would eliminate racism because discrimination harms those who engage in that behavior. Many economists today believe this to be true. However, Becker's theory assumes discrimination happens consciously and at the individual level. For example, according to Becker's theory, a store owner who is racist and refuses to hire African Americans will suffer financially. That's because this theory also assumes racists are in the minority. The racist store owner would lose money when other nonracist store owners hired African Americans at lower wages.

IMPLICIT BIAS

Racist attitudes and actions are not always explicit or overt. Implicit biases are attitudes and stereotypes that are formed unconsciously. Everyone has them, but people are often unaware of their own implicit biases. Scientists believe implicit biases are formed because of the brain's tendency to categorize the world in terms of "us versus them."

However, history shows that the free-market economy failed to eradicate discrimination based on race. Political economists argue this occurred because discrimination also happens on an institutional level—and changing these institutions is often very costly. For example, when a person of color enters a field that was previously exclusive to white men, there is more job competition. This often causes productivity among workers to plummet. In that case, bosses conclude that integration is costlier than maintaining discrimination.

Institutional economists look specifically at history and how racism was legitimized. The government, the economy, and public organizations of all types contributed to racism. These institutions can promote or inhibit economic growth, and the racism present within affects individuals' everyday lives.

| DISCUSSION STARTERS |

- Sometimes racism offers an economic benefit to the racist group. How might this encourage racism to continue?

- How do cartels challenge the ideals of a free-market economy?

- What roles can the government play in eliminating economic racism?

- Do businesspeople have obligations to their clients? If so, does this include catering to racist opinions or other requests that may be considered unethical?

| CHAPTER FOUR |

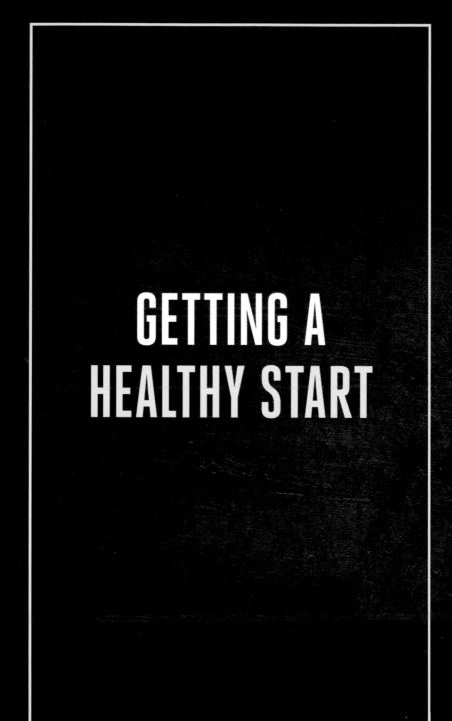

GETTING A HEALTHY START

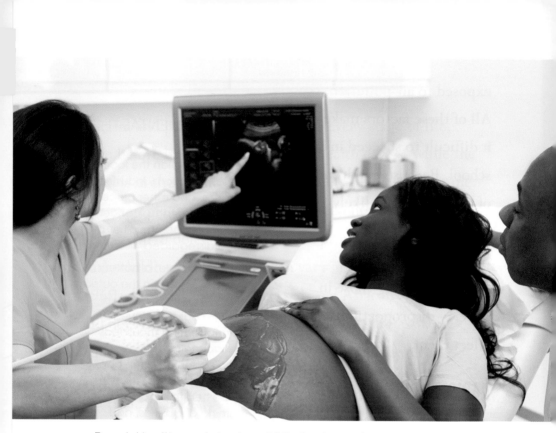

Prenatal health care is key to a child's development.

care providers may be the victims of their own implicit biases, which are subconscious beliefs that affect people even though they are not aware of their feelings. One program tested millions of people for implicit bias. Seventy to 80 percent of people who took the test showed a preference for white people.[3] This bias in favor of white people is found even in nonwhites and among people who believe themselves to be without prejudice. Some groups have started programs to help medical professionals overcome their implicit biases. Getting health-care workers to understand and overcome their subconscious prejudices could lead to better health care for minorities.

Poverty may also be a factor in unequal health care. When people are poor and do not have a convenient doctor, they are more likely to put off needed care. For example, Hispanic adults are 14 percent less likely than white adults to have had a health-care visit in the previous year.[4] African American adults are 11 percent less likely than white adults to have seen a dentist in the past 12 months.[5]

A health-care facility's location is usually the primary factor in determining whether someone receives good health care. Facilities located in poor communities typically offer worse health care. And because minorities

THE HEALTH INSURANCE GAP

Disparities in health care affect racial groups throughout life. Minorities are more likely to work in low-paying jobs that do not provide health care. With no employer-provided health care and no money to pay for health insurance, they have been more likely than white people to be uninsured.

Medicaid, a government health insurance program, provides insurance for some needy people, especially children. However, individual states have some control over who is eligible for Medicaid. Some states have provided aid only to people in poverty, while many other people have incomes that are above the poverty level but not high enough to afford traditional health insurance. In addition, many legal immigrants face a five-year waiting period or other restrictions to Medicaid access.

Doctors may have racial biases without being aware of them.

are more likely to live in poor communities, they receive worse health care.

Other factors might also contribute to different health-care results. People whose first language is not English are less likely to seek care, and they may struggle to communicate with doctors or to understand advice. Also, some groups have higher risks of certain diseases. For instance, Somali women are prone to vitamin D deficiencies, which can contribute to several serious health problems. Vitamin D deficiency can be determined by a test. However, medical training generally focuses on the most common problems that affect the majority of the population. Conditions that primarily affect minority groups may not get as much attention or awareness.

Doctors may miss warning signs or give advice that is not best suited to someone of a specific race or culture.

THE ECONOMIC IMPACTS

People who receive substandard or no health care are more likely to be in poor health. And those with poor health are not able to be as productive as those in good health. In the United States, the amount a person earns is typically tied to productivity. A person in poor health with a low productivity rate cannot expect to have the same job opportunities as someone in good health with a high productivity rate. As a result, a person in poor health must usually accept a lower-paying job.

Those with lower-paying jobs have less money to spend on health care—and health care is expensive. Insurance costs alone averaged $235 per person per month in 2013. For people with

COST OF HEALTH-CARE DISPARITIES

Health-care disparities for African Americans affect the economy directly and indirectly. From 2003 to 2006, African Americans spent more than $135 billion in excess medical costs. The discrepancies in illness and premature death for African Americans during the same time period also resulted in a total loss of more than $780 billion to the economy. This figure becomes even larger when including other minorities. When Hispanic people are added to the equation, the economy lost more than $1 trillion.[6]

low incomes, these costs eat up a significant percentage of their monthly expenses.[7]

Adults in poverty also die, on average, seven to eight years earlier than those with incomes at least four times above the poverty line.[8] When adults in poverty die so much earlier, they are able to work for fewer years. This makes it difficult to build up any wealth that could be passed on to future generations. Consequently, children will likely face the same obstacles as their parents. This continues a cycle in which poverty leads to poor health, and poor health leads to poverty.

TARGETING PROBLEMS

Ensuring that everyone has proper health care is important for giving people of every race equal opportunities in life. Several federal programs are working to eliminate the racial discrepancies in health care. The Centers for Disease Control and Prevention has partnered with local health departments to target neighborhoods that have high rates of certain diseases. Outreach programs provide education and support specific to those neighborhoods' needs. Another program involves updating standards to help people receive care in a language and cultural style they understand. Sometimes this means offering

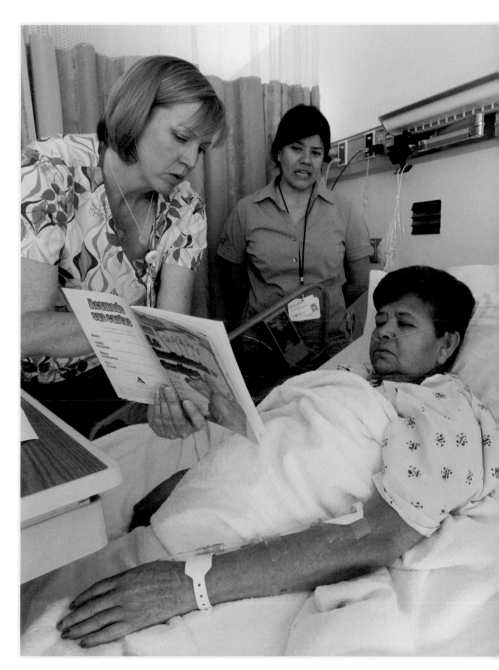

An interpreter, *center*, helps a patient understand the nurse's advice.

pamphlets in a language other than English or providing an interpreter.

Some hospitals are tracking patient results based on race. This can identify areas in which people of a certain race or culture need changes in treatment. For example, AnMed Health in Anderson, South Carolina, studied patient satisfaction and treatment success rates. In some cases, race made little difference. But the hospital made an important discovery about African Americans who had heart attacks. After the initial treatment, they were readmitted over the next 30 days at a much higher rate than other patients. By studying the problem and introducing intervention programs, the hospital was able to reduce the gap of readmittance between African Americans and other races within the first year.

A study at Massachusetts General Hospital in Boston, Massachusetts, found that Latinos were much less likely to get screened for colorectal cancer than white people were. The hospital interviewed Latino patients to determine what was preventing them from getting screened. With that information, the hospital was able to provide appropriate educational materials, scheduling services, and emotional support.

| DISCUSSION STARTERS |

- How does poverty play a part in an individual's health? How does this affect that person's ability to be successful in school?

- What are some ways health-care professionals might fail to adequately treat minorities? What contributes to these failures?

- How can medical schools address the problems of unequal health care? How can hospitals and other medical facilities address the problems?

- Government programs help millions of people avoid poverty. What might be some advantages and disadvantages of expanding or reducing these programs?

CHAPTER FIVE

EDUCATION AND CAREER OPPORTUNITIES

Preschool helps children build the skills they will need to be successful in grade school.

FINDING EDUCATIONAL SUCCESS

Racial disparities in education do not end once a child is old enough to attend public school. Schools in which the student population is made up mainly of minorities have less funding than schools where the majority of students are white. Because white students are more likely to come from higher-income families and live in more affluent neighborhoods, taxpayers living in those neighborhoods are able to devote more money to those school districts.

However, the difference in neighborhood incomes does not completely account for the discrepancies in school funding. School districts with less funding from taxpayers often receive money from state governments to help make up the difference. Statistics verify that poorer school districts receive more state aid than richer school districts do. But when a school district qualifies for state aid, it receives significantly more money when it has a higher proportion of white students. The schools low-income white children attend are, on average, better funded than the schools low-income children of color attend.

The educational system has been trying for years to find ways to close the gap between poor and rich students. Some practices have shown results. Full-service community schools attempt to provide not only education for the students but also health, social, and academic services for families and communities. Students may receive mentoring, job training, and career counseling. In addition, students receive access to health care, dental care, and nutrition services. Parents are also encouraged to get involved in students' academic lives and to further their own educations. This can include learning to read and write or learning English as a second language. The schools help families access social service programs. These schools may run food pantries to fight hunger or provide services such as free haircuts. They also encourage students to give back by becoming mentors to younger children.

Some schools offer free breakfasts, which help students stay alert and focused during the day.

Programs such as these cost money. The US Department of Education provides some funding to full-service community schools. Many of these expanded educational programs could not survive without financial help from the government. The federal government can help schools in poor neighborhoods that may not get enough funding from local taxes.

LEGACY ADMISSIONS

A good primary and high school education is important for preparing young people for successful lives. College is another key factor. Having a college degree dramatically increases the amount of money a person is likely to accumulate over his or her lifetime. Someone with a college degree earns an average of $19,500 per year more than someone with only a high school degree.[5] College can be quite expensive, however. The more wealth parents have, the more likely their children are to attend and finish college. Parents who went to college are also more likely to have children who go to college.

Legacy admissions policies also primarily benefit white middle- or upper-income or rich students. Legacy applicants are those who have family ties to an institution—typically one or both parents attended the college. Many colleges favor these legacy students, studies

A SCHOOL FAMILY

For some students, a community school becomes a second family when things are difficult at home. Khalil Bridges, a student at Renaissance Academy High School in Baltimore, Maryland, said he thought of the community school coordinator as a mother. She helped him remember deadlines and appointments while his own mother suffered from an illness that impaired her memory. He declared, "If you don't come to school, you're going to feel bad. That is where the people you call your family are."[6]

ATTENDANCE RATES

A study by the University of California–Berkeley looked at college attendance rates by race, but adjusted for parental wealth. The study found that for the wealthiest Americans, black students were actually more likely to attend a four-year college than were white students.

show. At 30 elite colleges, legacy students were 45 percent more likely to gain admission. Having a parent who attended the college was equal to an extra 160 points on the SAT (a standardized test), or approximately a 10 percent advantage.[7]

Legacy applicants may also benefit from special programs, such as webinars and consultations, to help them apply. One study found that Harvard University admitted more than 40 percent of legacy applicants, compared to only 11 percent of non-legacy applicants.[8] Approximately three-fourths of all liberal arts colleges and research institutions in the United States consider legacy status in their admissions decisions.[9]

COLLEGE FOR ALL

Some colleges try to provide additional opportunities for people of color by considering race as a factor in deciding which students to accept. This can help more minorities attend college, especially those who are not likely to benefit from legacy admissions. Race-based admissions account for roughly 25 percent of undergraduate admissions.[10] But some white students have challenged this practice, claiming it is reverse discrimination. In the 2003 case *Grutter v. Bollinger*, the US Supreme Court examined the admissions policy of the University of Michigan Law School. The school used race as one factor in deciding whether to admit applicants, giving an advantage to minorities. The court declared this policy

Many African Americans have benefited from policies that help people of color get accepted to universities.

CHAPTER SIX

NETWORKING FOR WORK

Differences in opportunities from early childhood through college explain some of the different rates of economic success between racial groups. However, even minorities who successfully earn advanced college degrees struggle to find equal success on the job. White people with an advanced degree earn substantially more on average than African Americans or Latinos with the same level of education.

This is in part because the same favoritism that helps legacy students get into elite schools extends to the workplace. Many top corporate firms primarily hire workers from elite schools. They may assume that the best students will always attend those schools. However, when a large percentage of admissions slots go to legacy students, this bias works toward keeping success in families that have already been successful. First-generation college students, or those whose parents did not attend elite universities, do not get the same opportunities.

Additional social factors work against the free-market ideal that everyone should be properly rewarded for his or her personal hard work. Finding a good job depends on several elements, but successful networking can play a large part. Many people find jobs and other opportunities through exchanging information with social contacts.

If someone has a large network of contacts who have good jobs and social power, that person is more likely to find high-paying employment. Upper-income and middle-income people with advanced educations tend to have the most effective networks. Parents in these groups can share their networks with their children.

In contrast, poorly educated parents living in low-income neighborhoods typically do not have powerful networks. Networking therefore tends to keep families in place, with children living in the same neighborhoods and working in jobs similar to those of their

WHAT IS COLLEGE WORTH?

College-educated people of every race earn more money and accumulate more wealth than those without college degrees. However, a college degree does not guarantee equal earnings. One study looked at the wealth of college graduates between 1992 and 2013 (when adjusted for inflation). For white Americans with college degrees, their wealth rose approximately 86 percent over the span of those 21 years. Wealth for Asian Americans rose almost 90 percent. Meanwhile, the wealth of African Americans who finished college dropped nearly 56 percent. Wealth for college-educated Hispanics fell 72 percent. In addition, the unemployment rate among African Americans was twice as high as the rate for whites, even among college graduates.[1]

Explaining these gaps is difficult. African Americans and Latinos are more likely to have large debt from college loans or buying a house, which affects their overall wealth. More debt also means less money to invest. Finally, having less wealth also leaves a person more vulnerable during times of economic scarcity.

parents. For instance, a banker's child has a much better chance of getting a job at the bank than the janitor's child does, regardless of each child's abilities.

FEEDBACK LOOPS

A positive feedback loop is a situation in which success leads to more success. For example, when Microsoft became a successful software company, it held a

Parents with low-income jobs are often unable to help their children find higher-paying jobs.

disproportionate amount of power in the technology industry. The company pressured computer manufacturers to use Microsoft software. As a result, consumers became more familiar with Microsoft and its software, and they expected the same software on their next computer. Each success led to more success.

Something similar happens in families. A wealthy family passes its wealth down to the next generation—not only directly, but also in terms of helping children reach success. Wealthy people can send their children to better high schools and then better colleges. These advantages can increase their children's earning potential and future wealth. Over time, the adult children can afford to buy homes in wealthy neighborhoods. Such neighborhoods tend to have more useful interpersonal networks. And these social networks lead to better jobs and other advantages.

White people, on average, have had advantages in education and jobs for centuries. An extreme example is wealthy white slaveholders and enslaved African Americans. When slavery was abolished, in theory both groups were equal. However, the former slaveholders retained much of their wealth, while the people who had been enslaved started with nothing. Even without specific racist actions, such as keeping African Americans from buying homes in white neighborhoods, positive feedback loops would favor the white people who started with more wealth. As long as neighborhoods are largely segregated, those advantages stay in white neighborhoods.

HOME OWNERSHIP

Positive feedback loops help explain why white people own five times the wealth that African Americans and Latinos do. Whites are more likely to be homeowners, with 73 percent owning homes compared with 45 percent of African Americans and 46 percent of Latino households. That is in part because white families are more likely to help their children buy homes. Twenty-seven percent of white young adults get parental help in making a down payment to purchase a home. Only 7 percent of African Americans get help—and they may receive less money, which means they cannot buy the same quality of home or buy it as early in life.[3]

A person's age when buying a home can matter a great deal. When home values rose dramatically in the 1970s, white homeowners grew richer. This occurred because white people wanted to live in predominantly white neighborhoods, whereas African American families in segregated neighborhoods did not see the same rise in home values. Rising home values helped white families move into better neighborhoods with well-financed public schools, so their children had better educations. The more expensive neighborhoods had wealthy neighbors, improving networking. All these factors added up to a boost for the next generation.

Meanwhile, in nonwhite neighborhoods, families owned smaller, older homes that were worth less. They had less money to share with their children for a college education or a down payment on a new home. And because local property taxes help fund schools, poorer neighborhoods often had worse schools.

Minorities suffered from a negative feedback loop. In a negative feedback loop, each disadvantage leads to more

Vacant homes in a neighborhood can cause property values to decrease.

disadvantages. Feedback loops help keep each group in its current place. As a result of these feedback loops, people in poor communities have a harder time getting good jobs, even when employers are not intentionally discriminating. Many communities are largely segregated by race, and minorities more often live in poor communities, so these social factors hurt minorities.

Despite the power of feedback loops, not all children stay in the same socioeconomic status as their parents. Over time, some wealthy families lose money through bad decisions or bad luck, while some poor children grow up to be successful due to hard work or good luck. In theory, it is possible that racial gaps between rich and poor will close over time. However, those in poverty tend to stay in poverty, and wealthy families tend to grow richer. Because of a history of segregation and unfair practices, minorities make up a disproportionate percentage of poor families. To close this gap, minorities need extra access to colleges and jobs if they do not have strong social networks.

DISCUSSION STARTERS

- What part does networking play in finding a good job? Do you think networking is a fair practice?

- How do feedback loops tend to keep poor people in poverty and keep wealthy people rich? How can these feedback loops be disrupted? Do you believe they should be disrupted?

SEGREGATION IN HOUSING

Segregation has been illegal in the United States for more than 50 years. However, many American cities remain largely segregated. One method of analyzing a city's segregation level uses a scale from 0 to 100. Zero indicates complete integration, and 100 indicates complete segregation. Many large metropolitan areas in the United States have segregation numbers between 50 and 70.[4] Black neighborhoods are generally poorer, and white neighborhoods are generally richer.

This is partially the result of overt racism prevalent in America's past, which forced minorities into certain neighborhoods. However, Vanita Gupta, head of the civil rights division at the US Department of Justice, says racism in the housing market is ongoing: "Banks continue to build and structure their lending operations in a way that avoids or fails to meaningfully serve communities of color."[5]

The US Justice Department vowed to fight these institutional prejudices. However, it is harder to police individuals' racist behavior. For instance, some real estate agents will show black clients homes only in neighborhoods that are predominantly black. In 2012, the Department of Housing and Urban Development reported that minority homeowners are, on average, shown fewer options when they attempt to buy or rent homes.

Housing segregation usually has a negative impact on minorities.

74

community. While explicit racism is illegal according to federal laws, many communities remain segregated due to the historic legacy of racism and subtler forms of discrimination.

CHAPTER SEVEN

DIVERSITY CHALLENGES

In *The Anatomy of Racial Inequality*, published in 2002, economist Glenn C. Loury explored social factors that might affect economics. Loury suggested that "self-confirming stereotypes" explained some entrenched racism.[1] This starts with a stereotype about a group of people. The stereotype may not be true for individuals within the group. However, people may have no choice but to act in a way that seems to reflect the stereotype. For those who are privileged, such actions seem to provide evidence that the stereotype is true.

For example, taxi drivers may avoid stopping for African American men, believing a stereotype that black men are more likely to be robbers. This prejudice may prevent many African American men from seeking taxis, and those looking for transportation will find another means instead. Consequently, among the black men who persist in trying to catch taxis, a greater percentage of them will be criminals who rob the drivers. Thus, the stereotype becomes true because the taxi drivers believed in it.

Loury found similar examples across various parts of society, including education and auto sales. This kind of behavior can easily influence people looking for jobs. In many cities, minorities tend to live in poor neighborhoods that do not have good schools. Therefore, many minorities do not receive the same quality of education as their white neighbors. That means some of those minorities will be less prepared for the job market. Employers may see a white employee doing better than a minority employee. This is not due to the employees' race but to their education. Yet some employers may make conscious or subconscious assumptions about job applicants. They may assume a white applicant will be a better worker, looking only at race and not at education.

Black residents of New York City have had trouble getting taxis to stop for many years.

STEREOTYPING THE SELF

Stereotypes also affect the behavior of the people being stereotyped. Science has proven that race is not related to intelligence. Yet psychologists have revealed a concept known as stereotype threat. In one study, they had two groups of African American college students take the same exam. One group was told it was an intelligence test. The other group was told it was a problem-solving test. The group who believed their intelligence was being tested performed worse. They apparently believed or feared stereotypes about their own intelligence.

WHITE AS STANDARD

Networking tends to keep power and money within certain groups, and this remains true in the workplace. Leaders of top companies may feel that only people who have experienced the culture of an elite university will fit in at the company. Traditionally, those attending such schools have been white men. Workers with a similar background may understand one another more easily and work together more efficiently. Workers are more productive when they are comfortable. Therefore, it can be economically beneficial for some employers to discriminate; they have a business reason to hire more white men who will fit in.

This could be one reason why numerous studies have documented discrimination in the hiring process. In one study conducted by the National Bureau of Economic

Research, researchers sent out fake résumés and job applications. Half of the fake applicants were given names common in the black community; the other half were given white-sounding names. On average, the applicants with white-sounding names received 50 percent more callbacks than those with black-sounding names.[2]

When these employers do hire minorities, they tend to choose candidates who do not seem too different from the current majority of employees. In companies where white culture is the standard, minorities may face pressure to blend in as much as possible. To minimize their race, they may try to socialize strictly with white coworkers. They may try to eliminate any accent and avoid speaking any language other than English. They may dress and style their hair as similar as possible to their white coworkers.

For example, an African American woman could straighten her hair, wear it natural, or wear many braids or dreadlocks. Her choice influences how others will see her, including how much attention they pay to her race. The ability of people from minority groups to fit in may influence how they are treated on the job. If they avoid looking or behaving like the stereotype of their race, they reduce the risk of discrimination. However, they do so at a cost. They lose personal identity, racial group identity, and freedom of choice.

Hairstyles such as dreadlocks can be a major part of a person's identity.

In contrast, because white culture is usually accepted as the standard, white people do not have to adapt to their circumstances as often. If they are working in teams, it falls to the minorities to adapt in order to ensure everyone works together smoothly. The white people are unlikely to notice this happening. They can take it for granted that everyone is behaving in the "correct" way and complain when white standards are broken.

A minority who copies the majority standards may see personal benefits. However, the minority community as a whole does not benefit from that individual's success. Stereotypes remain, and minority cultures are repressed. People who minimize their own race may also be less likely to help other minorities. For example, successful African Americans may hesitate to mentor new black employees for fear of drawing attention to their own outsider status.

Meanwhile, when minority cultures are repressed, society does not benefit from true diversity in every field. Companies will compete to hire the few minorities who best fit white cultural standards. These may not be the most qualified employees in other ways. Minorities who are unwilling or unable to fit in may struggle to find jobs that make the best use of their potential.

SCARCITY AND THE BRAIN

Scientists, psychologists, and economists are currently studying how scarcity affects the brain. When a resource, such as money or time, becomes scarce, the brain hyperfocuses on it. This can seem to be a good thing in the short term. For example, deadlines can spur people to do an incredible amount of work in a short amount of time. But the long-term effects of scarcity are detrimental. By hyperfocusing on one aspect, the brain does not have enough mental bandwidth to attend to anything else, such as impulse control or long-term planning.

Minority workers, who are likely to have less wealth than their white coworkers, are more likely to start out their professional careers with a mental bandwidth that is already taxed by economic scarcity. This limited bandwidth can inhibit a person's productivity. To the average manager, it can seem as though white people are simply more productive than people of color.

PROMOTING DIVERSITY

Many people, companies, and institutions recognize the importance of fighting stereotypes and promoting diversity. Some large companies have instituted programs designed to increase diversity. In the beginning, these programs may have been inspired less by good intentions and more by a fear of lawsuits. In the late 1990s and early 2000s, companies in the financial industry lost several multimillion-dollar lawsuits for discrimination.

In response, many large companies began programs aimed at promoting the value of diversity. However, these programs have not shown much success in actually improving diversity. The proportion of African American men in management among all US companies with 100 or more employees rose from 3 percent to 3.3 percent from 1985 to 2014—a difference of only 0.3 percent over the course of three decades.[3]

The problem, according to a report in the *Harvard Business Review*, is that most diversity programs attempt to control how managers behave. Studies have shown that people often respond with anger, which they may turn against the minority groups. In fact, diversity programs can actually increase bias. Companies with mandatory training saw a 9 percent decrease in the number of female African American managers over the course of five years.[4]

Companies that offer voluntary training tend to have higher rates of success in increasing diversity in the workforce.

Voluntary training seems to work better than mandatory training. Voluntary training led to increases in the numbers of minorities in management positions: the number of Asian American men and women and African American and Hispanic men increased by 9 to 13 percent over five years.[5] One theory suggests voluntary training encourages people to think of themselves as proponents of diversity. In seeing themselves that way, they act to support diversity.

Other programs designed to increase diversity, such as testing all job applicants and using annual performance ratings, have also failed. They cannot overcome some managers' bias for white men, especially individuals they already know. One study found that hiring teams paid attention when women and African Americans did poorly on tests, but they ignored the failures of white men. The hiring teams could convince themselves they knew the white men were capable of doing better than their test scores showed, but they did not make the same assumptions about minorities and women. Thus, the tests hurt the people they were trying to protect. Performance reviews can also harm minorities through bias, and they have been shown not to increase diversity.

Grievance procedures are another failed tactic. These procedures allow employees to challenge decisions on pay, promotion, and termination if they believe racial or gender bias influenced the decision. However, many managers react to complaints by trying to get revenge on those who complain. They may ridicule or ignore these employees, demote them, or find other forms of punishment.

In 2015, 45 percent of complaints to the federal Equal Employment Opportunity Commission included

GROUP BEHAVIOR

Race is only one criterion people may use to form groups. In one experiment, a social psychologist studied boys who had been randomly assigned to groups at a summer camp. The boys quickly began favoring members of their own group. They competed against and acted hostile toward boys in other groups. But when the groups were asked to work together on a common goal, their behavior changed. Sharing a task encouraged cooperation and reduced competition and hostility.

a charge of retaliation. A fear of retaliation discourages people from speaking up when they experience or see discrimination. In turn, companies may believe they do not have a problem because they are not hearing complaints. The *Harvard Business Review* report found that the number of all minority groups in management, except Hispanic men, declined by 3 to 11 percent in the five years after companies adopted formal grievance systems. Furthermore, the number of white women in management declined as well.[6]

| DISCUSSION STARTERS |

- What are some stereotypes you have seen or experienced in your own life? Do you think there is ever any benefit to stereotypes? What can be done to challenge stereotypes?

- How do you think society's stereotypes affect individuals' views of themselves?

- Do you think people should be expected to conform to standards of dress and hairstyle at the workplace? What are the advantages and disadvantages? If workplace standards are set, should they accommodate racial diversity?

- People of color may believe the world is more racist than white people do. What might cause this difference in viewpoint?

THE FUTURE

There is no single way to determine the economic damage of racism. Many racial minorities have not received the education, training, and opportunities that would allow them to thrive. A 1993 study tried to determine the economic cost of not using African Americans in the workforce to their greatest potential. It estimated that the US economy lost approximately $241 billion per year. Many experts believe the number is much higher today—and higher still if other minorities are counted. Some experts believe the cost of racism could be as high as $1 trillion every year.[1]

New businesses that do not have entrenched roles along racial and gender lines can benefit from having a diverse population of workers. People from a variety of social and cultural backgrounds, regardless of race, can bring together diverse viewpoints to provide greater creativity.

Some fields especially benefit from having workers from different races, classes, and cultural backgrounds. For example, a police force may be more successful if officers come from the communities being policed. Social workers may be more successful if they understand the languages and cultures of groups in their communities. Students succeed more when teachers have a greater understanding and sympathy about students' backgrounds and experiences. These advantages do not depend specifically on race but rather on cultural experience and insight, which may be tied to race.

STEPS TO SUCCESS

Experts disagree on how best to close the racial economic gap. However, many think equal access to quality early childhood education is key. Children who grow up

Many police forces are beginning to recognize the value of diversity.

A recruiter, *right*, speaks to high school students at a college fair.

in poverty consistently perform worse in school than their more affluent peers. Programs such as Head Start are designed to intervene in the lives of children from low-income families. Many studies show Head Start can improve the intelligence of participating children. Other studies show programs such as Head Start can also have long-term health effects, leading to low incidences of heart disease and diabetes. However, despite this research, the United States still ranks 25th among 29 industrialized countries when it comes to investing in early childhood education.[2]

In the workplace, some programs have shown positive results in increasing diversity. One simple principle is

known as contact. The idea is that groups will be less biased when they interact with one another. This principle has been known since World War II (1939–1945). The US Army was originally segregated, but eventually African American platoons joined white companies. Surveys found that integrated companies had much lower racial hostility and a greater willingness to work together.

Contact lessens bias only when the groups work toward a common goal as equals; the principle doesn't work when roles are dramatically different, such as when minorities work as servants. In the business world, self-managed teams, in which a group of employees work together on projects, can provide this kind of contact.

Teams can bring together people from different parts of the company, such as sales, technology, and production. Each of these specialties may primarily have workers of one race, but the team brings them together. This helps break down stereotypes and leads to more equality in hiring and promotion.

Another successful tactic is known as engagement. This includes practices such as inviting managers to participate in college recruitment programs focused on diversity. Managers participate voluntarily, and the goal is positive: to find great potential employees. When companies start college recruitment programs targeting women and minorities, the number of women and minorities in management increases by up to 10 percent after five years.[3]

Asking managers to mentor minorities also helps reduce manager bias. White men in executive positions often do not feel

COMPOUNDING BENEFITS

Positive feedback loops mean initial increases in diversity can lead to even more diversity in the long term. After a race discrimination suit cost Coca-Cola $193 million in 2000, the company instituted recruitment and mentoring programs. This dramatically increased the representation of minorities among both salaried employees and managers. The cycle continued, and by 2016, Coca-Cola had 17 African American women in vice-president positions or higher, including the chief financial officer.[4]

comfortable reaching out to young men and women of color. However, when they are assigned mentees through official programs, they are often eager to participate. In addition, a mentee's success reflects well on the mentor. Mentoring programs can increase diversity by 10 percent or more.[5]

A final diversity tactic uses social accountability, which draws on people's desire to look good in front of others. This can involve a variety of practices. At one firm, African Americans regularly received smaller raises than white employees, even when they had the same job and performance ratings. Then the firm began publicly posting average performance ratings and pay raises for each unit, identified by race and gender. The gaps largely disappeared once managers knew others would be able to see their biases.

Diversity task forces can also encourage social accountability. These groups look for solutions to problems, encouraging everyone to get involved. Participating in diversity programs helps people look good, so the employees are more likely to volunteer. Meanwhile, if they know others are watching and they might have to explain biased decisions, they are less likely to act on a bias they may have. Within five years of starting diversity task forces, most companies see

9 to 30 percent increases in the representation of each minority group.[6]

Despite the promise of these tactics, fewer than 15 percent of US firms have college recruitment programs for minorities, while only 10 percent have mentoring programs. Approximately one-third use self-managed teams. Only 20 percent of employers at medium- and large-sized companies use diversity task forces.[7] All of these solutions could be much more widespread, helping close the success gap between the races.

SMALL BUT DIVERSE

Many economic studies do not consider American Indians because their population is so small. American Indians make up approximately 2 percent of the population and 1 percent of the labor force.[8] When American Indians are factored into economic studies, they are all lumped together, despite the fact that the 5.2 million American Indians in the United States come from hundreds of different tribes.[9] The average income for an American Indian belonging to a gaming reservation is higher than the average income for an American Indian belonging to a nongaming reservation, for example.

UNIQUE SOLUTIONS

There is no single plan that will successfully combat economic racism for every company, organization, and community. Solutions will vary by racial group and other circumstances. For example, some studies have looked at employment rates for different American Indian tribes. Employment is higher where there is strong tribal leadership that draws on cultural traditions. Leadership set up by the US government was less successful in increasing employment. In addition, many tribes have access to natural resources such as timber and valuable minerals. Government policies may limit how tribes can develop those resources. Changes in the way the federal government manages reservations could allow for more development.

Employment rates also vary considerably by state. Contributing factors may include the average age of American Indians in that state, educational opportunities, and whether the tribe

AMERICAN INDIANS AND JOBS

In 2016, American Indians had unemployment levels of approximately 11 percent, nearly double that of the overall US average. Some nations had unemployment in excess of 60 percent. Disparities in the educational system mean a lower percentage of students finish public high school or complete college. American Indians also suffer from job discrimination. When compared with white Americans of similar gender, age, location, and education level, American Indian employment was 31 percent lower.[10] The situation is especially difficult for the 22 percent of American Indians and Alaska Natives who live on reservations.[11] While the federal government provides health and educational assistance to reservations, finding employment is difficult. Few jobs are available on reservations, so people have to leave their home regions to find work. That may mean leaving family behind, while paying higher transportation costs to commute long distances.

itself hires many employees. For instance, the Tlingits and Haidas are major employers in Southeast Alaska. According to a 2013 study, the Tlingit-Haida nations had the highest employment rate of any American Indian nation, at 75.8 percent.[12]

Meanwhile, reservations often lack access to financial services such as credit. Some tribes have local community funds that provide small loans to businesses and individuals. These loans allow American Indians to start or expand their own businesses. The solutions for American Indians must be tailored to each nation's specific circumstances. Other racial groups and communities will also need unique solutions.

The 2008 election of Barack Obama was the first time Americans elected a black person to the highest office in the United States. John McWhorter, an African American associate professor at Columbia University, wrote a commentary in 2010 suggesting the United States is "post-racial." He claimed, "Obama's first year has shown us again and again that race does not matter in America the way it used to. We've come more than a mere long way—we're almost there."[13]

However, a measure of progress is typically followed by a period of backlash. Current statistics also show the United States is not post-racial. Individual success is still tied to race and even more to family wealth or poverty. The United States is not yet the land of equal opportunity for all. More economic studies are needed to provide greater insight into what works and what does not in terms of combating racism and improving diversity at colleges and in the workplace. Armed with this information, individuals, businesses, and organizations can work toward a future that lives up to equal opportunities for all.

| DISCUSSION STARTERS |

- What are some ways a business or organization might benefit from having people from diverse backgrounds? Is this more important in some fields than in others?

- Do you believe it is important to study the success rates of diversity programs? Why or why not?

- Do you think race still matters in the United States? Has this changed over the past century, and is it changing now?

- What do you think people and governments should do to improve economic equality in the future?

ESSENTIAL FACTS

SIGNIFICANT EVENTS

- The American Civil War ended in 1865, and slavery was officially abolished. African Americans could no longer be held as slaves, but many started their emancipation without any wealth.

- The United States' involvement in World War I and World War II changed the labor market, so some African Americans moved into traditionally white jobs.

- In the 1920s through the 1960s, racial deed restrictions were common, preventing houses in many neighborhoods from being sold to people of color.

- In 1965, the US government created the Head Start early childhood education program to try to close the achievement gap between white students and students of color.

KEY PLAYERS

- Gary Becker published his neoclassical economic theory of discrimination in 1955. The theory asserts that the free market will eliminate discrimination based on race and gender. Many people still believe this theory to be true.

- The Economic Policy Institute was founded in 1986 as a nonpartisan think tank, committed to exploring the needs of low- and middle-income workers in the United States.

- The US Supreme Court upheld race-based college admission processes in *Grutter v. Bollinger* in 2003.

IMPACT ON SOCIETY

At the end of the American Civil War, different racial groups were supposed to have equal economic opportunities. However, people of different ethnicities did not have equal amounts of wealth. In particular, African Americans had not been allowed to accrue money while they were enslaved. Furthermore, institutions such as governments and the economy were shaped by the racism prevalent in the 1800s, and its influence continued in the decades that followed. Unequal access to high-quality education, housing, and health care has negatively affected the economic opportunities for people of color, particularly African Americans. Activists today work to highlight the wealth gap that exists between white adults and people of color and suggest ways that it could be narrowed.

QUOTE

"In America the children of affluent parents grow up to be affluent, and the children of the poor remain poor."

—*Economic Policy Institute*

GLOSSARY

BOYCOTT
A refusal to have dealings with another group, usually in order to express disapproval or to force acceptance of certain conditions.

DISCRIMINATION
Unfair treatment of other people, usually because of race, age, or gender.

FEEDBACK LOOP
A situation in which the outcome encourages more of the same outcome, either positive or negative.

FREE MARKET
An economic system in which wages and prices are determined by competition, without government regulation.

INSTITUTIONAL
Having to do with an established law or practice in a society.

INTEGRATION
Acceptance of people belonging to different groups (such as races) as equals in society.

MARKET FORCES

The economic factors that affect the price, demand, and availability of a product or service.

NETWORKING

The act of exchanging information and help.

REPRESS

To hold back a thought or emotion or to force painful memories into the unconscious.

SEGREGATION

The practice of separating groups of people based on race, gender, ethnicity, or other factors.

SOCIOECONUMIC

Related to both social and economic factors.

STEREOTYPE

A widely held but oversimplified idea about a particular type of person or thing.

SUPREMACIST

Someone who believes people of a particular race, religion, or other category are better than other people.

ADDITIONAL RESOURCES

SELECTED BIBLIOGRAPHY

Carbado, Devon W., and Mitu Gulati. "The Law and Economics of Critical Race Theory." *Yale Law Journal* 112.7 (2003). Print.

Ramirez, Steven. "What We Teach When We Teach about Race: The Problem of Law and Pseudo-economics." *Journal of Legal Education* 54.3 (2004). Print.

Roithmayr, Daria. *Reproducing Racism*. New York: New York UP, 2014. Print.

FURTHER READINGS

Mayer, David A., and Melanie E. Fox. *The Everything Economics Book: From Theory to Practice, Your Complete Guide to Understanding Economics*. Avon, MA: Adams Media, 2010. Print.

Tarrant-Reid, Linda. *Discovering Black America: From the Age of Exploration to the Twenty-First Century*. New York: Abrams, 2012. Print.

WEBSITES

To learn more about Race in America, visit **abdobooklinks.com**. These links are routinely monitored and updated to provide the most accurate information available.

FOR MORE INFORMATION

For more information on this subject, contact or visit the following organizations:

THE MUSEUM OF TOLERANCE
9786 W. Pico Boulevard
Los Angeles, CA 90035
310-772-2505
http://www.museumoftolerance.com/

This multimedia museum is designed to examine racism and prejudice around the world. The museum has a strong focus on the history of the Holocaust but also covers civil rights and other eras.

NAACP
4805 Mt. Hope Drive
Baltimore, MD 21215
877-NAACP-98
http://www.naacp.org

The mission of the National Association for the Advancement of Colored People (NAACP) is to ensure the political, educational, social, and economic equality of rights of all persons and to eliminate race-based discrimination. Each state has a local branch.

NATIONAL MUSEUM OF AFRICAN AMERICAN HISTORY AND CULTURE
1400 Constitution Avenue NW
Washington, DC 20560
844-750-3012
https://nmaahc.si.edu/

This national museum is devoted to the documentation of African American life, history, and culture. Exhibits cover slavery, segregation, the civil rights era, and many more aspects of history.

SOURCE NOTES

CHAPTER 1. STARTING POINTS

1. Eileen Patten and Jens Manual Krogstad. "Black Child Poverty Rate Holds Steady, Even as Other Groups See Declines." *Pew Research Center*. Pew Research Center, 14 July 2015. Web. 10 Mar. 2017.

2. Bernadette D. Proctor, Jessica L. Semega, and Melissa A. Kollar. "Income and Poverty in the United States: 2015." *US Census Bureau*. US Department of Commerce, 13 Sept. 2016. Web. 10 Mar. 2017.

3. "Poverty Thresholds." *US Census Bureau*. US Department of Commerce, 13 Feb. 2017. Web. 10 Mar. 2017.

4. Bernadette D. Proctor, Jessica L. Semega, and Melissa A. Kollar. "Income and Poverty in the United States: 2015." *US Census Bureau*. US Department of Commerce, 13 Sept. 2016. Web. 10 Mar. 2017.

5. "Living Conditions." *Native American Aid*. Native American Aid, n.d. Web. 10 Mar. 2017.

6. "The Poverty Cycle." *Running Strong for American Indian Youth*. Running Strong for American Indian Youth, n.d. Web. 10 Mar. 2017.

7. Algernon Austin. "Native Americans and Jobs: The Challenge and the Promise." *Economic Policy Institute*. Economic Policy Institute, 17 Dec. 2013. Web. 10 Mar. 2017.

CHAPTER 2. ECONOMICS AND HISTORY

1. Janelle Jones. "The Racial Wealth Gap: How African-Americans Have Been Shortchanged out of the Materials to Build Wealth." *Economic Policy Institute*. Economic Policy Institute, 13 Feb. 2017. Web. 10 Mar. 2017.

2. "Workers of the Central Pacific Railroad." *PBS*. PBS, n.d. Web. 10 Mar. 2017.

3. "Chinese Immigration and the Transcontinental Railroad." *United States Citizenship*. USCitizenship.info, n.d. Web. 10 Mar. 2017.

CHAPTER 3. RACISM IN AMERICAN SOCIETY

1. Lauren Kirchner. "Cross Burning Is More Common Than You Think." *Pacific Standard*. Pacific Standard, 14 Jan 2014. Web. 10 Mar. 2017.

2. "Racial Restrictive Covenants." *Seattle Civil Rights & Labor History Project*. University of Washington, n.d. Web. 10 Mar. 2017.

CHAPTER 4. GETTING A HEALTHY START

1. Algernon Austin. "Native Americans and Jobs: The Challenge and the Promise." *Economic Policy Institute*. Economic Policy Institute, 17 Dec. 2013. Web. 10 Mar. 2017.

2. Alexander Nazaryan. "In Southeast Los Angeles, Your Front Yard Might Be a Toxic Waste Site." *Newsweek*. Newsweek, 6 Apr. 2016. Web. 10 Mar. 2017.

3. "Q&A with the Authors of Blindspot." *Blindspot*. Blindspot, n.d. Web. 10 Mar. 2017.

4. Samantha Artiga, et al. "Key Facts on Health and Health Care by Race and Ethnicity." *Kaiser Family Foundation*. Kaiser Family Foundation, June 2016. Web. 10 Mar. 2017.

5. Ibid.

6. Thomas A. LaVeist, Darrell J. Gaskin, and Patrick Richard. "The Economic Burden of Health Inequalities in the United States." *Joint Center for Political and Economic Studies*. Health Forum, Sept. 2009. Web. 10 Mar. 2017.

7. "Average Monthly Premiums Per Person in the Individual Market." *Kaiser Family Foundation*. Kaiser Family Foundation, n.d. Web. 10 Mar. 2017.

8. Claire Conway. "Poor Health: When Poverty Becomes Disease." *University of California San Francisco*. Regents of the University of California, 6 Jan. 2016. Web. 10 Mar. 2017.

9. Sydney Lupkin. "Deep Roots for Lack of Minorities in American Medical Schools." *MedPage Today*. MedPage Today, 15 March 2016. Web. 10 Mar. 2017.

CHAPTER 5. EDUCATION AND CAREER OPPORTUNITIES

1. Algernon Austin. "Native Americans and Jobs: The Challenge and the Promise." *Economic Policy Institute*. Economic Policy Institute, 17 Dec. 2013. Web. 10 Mar. 2017.

2. "Preschool and Kindergarten Enrollment." *National Center for Education Statistics*. US Department of Education, May 2016. Web. 10 Mar. 2017.

3. Ibid.

4. Grover J. "Russ" Whitehurst. "Can We Be Hard-Headed about Preschool? A Look at Head Start." *Brookings*. Brookings Institution, 16 Jan. 2013. Web. 10 Mar. 2017.

5. Daria Roithmayr. *Reproducing Racism*. New York: New York UP, 2014. Print. 64–65.

6. "Graduating from a Community School." *Coalition for Community Schools*. Coalition for Community Schools at the Institute for Educational Leadership, n.d. Web. 10 Mar. 2017.

7. Dave Bergman. "Does Being a 'Legacy' Increase Your Admission Odds?" *College Transitions*. College Transitions, 12 Mar 2015. Web. 10 Mar. 2017.

8. Steven A. Ramirez. "What We Teach When We Teach about Race: The Problem of Law and Pseudo-Economics." *Loyola University Chicago, School of Law*. Semantic Scholar, 2004. Web. 10 Mar. 2017.

9. Dave Bergman. "Does Being a 'Legacy' Increase Your Admission Odds?" *College Transitions*. College Transitions, 12 Mar 2015. Web. 10 Mar. 2017.

10. Ben Casselman. "Race Gap Narrows in College Enrollment, But Not in Graduation." *FiveThirtyEight*. FiveThirtyEight, 30 Apr. 2014. Web. 10 Mar. 2017.

11. "Grutter v. Bollinger et al." *Legal Information Institute*. Cornell University Law School, n.d. Web. 10 Mar. 2017.

12. Meredith Kolodner. "College Degree Gap Grows Wider between Whites, Blacks, and Latinos." *Hechinger Report*. Teachers College at Columbia University, 7 Jan. 2016. Web. 10 Mar. 2017.

SOURCE
NOTES CONTINUED

13. Ben Casselman. "Race Gap Narrows in College Enrollment, But Not in Graduation." *FiveThirtyEight*. FiveThirtyEight, 30 Apr. 2014. Web. 10 Mar. 2017.

CHAPTER 6. NETWORKING FOR WORK

1. Patricia Cohen. "Racial Wealth Gap Persists Despite Degree, Study Says." *New York Times*. New York Times Company, 16 Aug. 2015. Web. 10 Mar. 2017.

2. Estelle Sommeiller and Mark Price. "The Increasingly Unequal States of America." *Economic Policy Institute*. Economic Policy Institute, 26 Jan. 2015. Web. 10 Mar. 2017.

3. Daria Roithmayr. *Reproducing Racism*. New York: New York UP, 2014. Print. 63

4. Rajini Vaidyanathan. "Why Don't Black and White Americans Live Together?" *BBC News*. BBC News, 8 Jan. 2016. Web. 10 Mar. 2017.

5. "Justice News." *US Department of Justice*. US Department of Justice, 24 Sept. 2015. Web. 10 Mar. 2017.

CHAPTER 7. DIVERSITY CHALLENGES

1. Steven A. Ramirez. "What We Teach When We Teach about Race: The Problem of Law and Pseudo-Economics." *Loyola University Chicago, School of Law*. Semantic Scholar, 2004. Web. 10 Mar. 2017.

2. "Employers' Replies to Racial Names." *National Bureau of Economic Research*. National Bureau of Economic Research, n.d. Web. 10 Mar. 2017.

3. Frank Dobbin and Alexandra Kalev. "Why Diversity Programs Fail." *Harvard Business Review*. Harvard Business School Publishing, July–Aug. 2016. Web. 10 Mar. 2017.

4. Ibid.

5. Ibid.

6. Ibid.

CHAPTER 8. THE FUTURE

1. Steven A. Ramirez. "What We Teach When We Teach about Race: The Problem of Law and Pseudo-Economics." *Loyola University Chicago, School of Law.* Semantic Scholar, 2004. Web. 10 Mar. 2017.

2. "Can Early Childhood Interventions Improve Health and Well-Being?" *Robert Wood Johnson Foundation.* Robert Wood Johnson Foundation, Mar. 2016. Web. 10 Mar. 2017

3. Frank Dobbin and Alexandra Kalev. "Why Diversity Programs Fail." *Harvard Business Review.* Harvard Business School Publishing, July–Aug. 2016. Web. 10 Mar. 2017.

4. Ibid.

5. Ibid.

6. Ibid.

7. Ibid.

8. Katherine Peralta. "Native Americans Left Behind in the Economic Recovery." *US News & World Report.* US News & World Report, 27 Nov. 2014. Web. 10 Mar. 2017.

9. "Profile: American Indian/Alaska Native." *US Department of Health and Human Services.* US Department of Health and Human Services, n.d. Web. 10 Mar. 2017.

10. Katherine Peralta. "Native Americans Left Behind in the Economic Recovery." *US News & World Report.* US News & World Report, 27 Nov. 2014. Web. 10 Mar. 2017.

11. Ibid.

12. Algernon Austin. "Native Americans and Jobs: The Challenge and the Promise." *Economic Policy Institute.* Economic Policy Institute, 17 Dec. 2013. Web. 10 Mar. 2017.

13. John H. McWhorter. "It's Official: America Is 'Post-Racial' in the Age of Obama." *The Grio.* Manhattan Institute, 14 Jan. 2010. Web. 10 Mar. 2017.

INDEX

accountability, 95–96

American Civil War, 22, 24, 26–28

American Indians, 10–11, 42, 54, 96–98

Anatomy of Racial Inequality, The, 78

Asian Americans, 10, 26–27, 37, 67, 85

Becker, Gary, 37–38

Birth of a Nation, The, 35

California, 26, 43, 60

cartels, 32–34

Centers for Disease Control and Prevention, 48

Central Pacific Railroad, 26

Chicago, Illinois, 34

child care, 10

Chinese Immigrants, 26

Civil Rights Act of 1964, 34

Clansman, The, 35

clothing, 10

Coca-Cola, 94

competition, 22, 26, 32–34, 38, 86

contact, 92–94

debt, 20, 67

demand, 18–19, 22

Department of Education, US, 58

Department of Health and Human Services, US, 43, 55

Department of Justice, US, 74

discrimination, 11–12, 22, 25, 26, 28, 37–39, 81, 84, 87

    employment, 25, 72, 80, 94, 97

    housing, 74–75

    reverse discrimination, 61

diversity, 50, 62, 83, 84–87, 90, 92, 94–96, 99

Dixon, Thomas, 35

Economic Policy Institute, 20, 70

economics

    classical, 22

    institutional, 39

    neoclassical, 20–21

    political, 21

education, 8, 12–13, 16, 21, 36, 37, 48, 51, 54–63, 66–67, 69, 71, 78–79, 90

    college, 6–7, 12, 50, 59–60, 62–63, 66–67, 69, 71, 73, 80, 94, 96–97, 99

    early childhood, 54–55, 91–92, 97

    full-service community schools, 57–58

    funding of, 56–58

    medical school, 50

    quality of, 79

Elementary and Secondary Education Act, 55

engagement, 94–95

English Americans, 26

Equal Employment Opportunity Commission, 86–87

Every Student Succeeds Act, 55

feedback loops, 68–73, 94
Fifteenth Amendment, 28
free market, 22, 24, 27, 38, 66

Grutter v. Bollinger, 61
Gupta, Vanita, 74

Harvard Business Review, 84, 87
Head Start, 55, 92
health care, 13, 42, 43–48, 57
health insurance, 17, 45, 47
Hispanic Americans, 8, 10–11, 43, 45, 47, 50–51, 55, 62, 66–67, 70, 85, 87
home ownership, 34–35, 67, 70–74
housing, 10–11, 13, 23, 74–75

implicit bias, 38, 44
income, 10, 13, 20, 32, 37, 43, 45, 48, 54–57, 59, 62–63, 67, 70, 92, 96
Indian Health Service, 42
Irish Americans, 26–27

Jewish Americans, 37
Jim Crow laws, 24, 28–29

Ku Klux Klan, 35

labor unions, 22–23, 33
Latin Americans. *See* Hispanic Americans
legacy admissions, 59–60
Levittown, 25
Loury, Glenn C., 78

markets, 16, 18, 23, 32, 79
Medicaid, 45
Microsoft, 68–69

National Bureau of Economic Research, 80–81
New York City, 27

Obama, Barack, 11, 98
O'Connor, Sandra Day, 62

poverty, 7–8, 10–11, 13, 35, 42–43, 45, 48, 54

racism, 10, 12–13, 16, 22–23, 26–27, 32–33, 35, 37–39, 42–43, 69, 74–75, 78, 90, 96, 99

scarcity, 19, 67, 83
segregation, 24, 34–35, 42, 70–75, 93
slavery, 22, 27, 28, 69
Somali Americans, 46
stereotype threat, 80
stereotypes, 38, 78, 80–82, 84, 94
supply, 18–19, 22, 32
Supreme Court, US, 61–62

transportation, 10, 78, 97

unemployment, 11–12, 16, 20, 63, 67, 97

voter suppression, 28–29
Voting Rights Act of 1965, 29

wealth, 16, 20, 36, 48, 59, 60, 67, 69–71, 73, 75, 83, 99
World War I, 32
World War II, 93

ABOUT THE AUTHOR

M. M. Eboch writes about science, history, and culture for all ages. Her recent nonfiction titles include *Chaco Canyon*, *Living with Dyslexia*, and *The Green Movement*. Writing as Chris Eboch, her novels for young people include *The Eyes of Pharaoh*, a mystery in ancient Egypt; *The Well of Sacrifice*, a Mayan adventure; *The Genie's Gift*, a Middle Eastern fantasy; and the Haunted series, which starts with *The Ghost on the Stairs*.